TEACH YOURSELF TO PLAY
GUITAR

by David M. Brewster

T0055316

Don't delay, start today!

This book provides a quick, effective, un-complicated, and practical method to playing guitar. Get started right away and learn at your own pace in the comfort of your home.

ALSO AVAILABLE:

Teach Yourself to Play
Guitar
Book/Audio HL00696029

Teach Yourself to Play
Guitar Chords
Book/Audio HL00144128

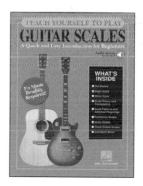

Teach Yourself to Play
Guitar Scales
Book/Audio HL00160293

ISBN 978-0-634-06540-8

Visit Hal Leonard Online at
www.halleonard.com

World headquarters, contact:
Hal Leonard
7777 West Bluemound Road
Milwaukee, WI 53213
Email: info@halleonard.com

In Europe, contact:
Hal Leonard Europe Limited
1 Red Place
London, W1K 6PL
Email: info@halleonardeurope.com

In Australia, contact:
Hal Leonard Australia Pty. Ltd.
4 Lentara Court
Cheltenham, Victoria, 3192 Australia
Email: info@halleonard.com.au

Introduction

Congratulations on your decision to play the guitar! You've chosen the perfect book to begin your musical journey. With this book you will need no prior music knowledge or experience—you don't even have to read music! *Teach Yourself to Play Guitar* teaches by way of easily interpreted tablature ("tab") enhanced with user-friendly rhythm notation. Bottom line: You can start playing now!

This book opens with essential basics like guitar anatomy, hand and finger placement, and posture, as well as a concise overview on how to read and interpret chord charts, tab, and rhythm notation. It then introduces the student to power chords, open-position chords, single-note patterns (scales, fills, arpeggios), and barre chords. Each section incorporates music examples from a wide variety of musical genres, including well-known and immediately recognizable melodies and songs.

The objective of this book is not only to get the beginning guitarist playing immediately but also to lay the foundation for a growing repertoire upon which the student can build. The musical examples and songs were carefully designed or chosen, and then methodically organized, so as to quickly and thoroughly acclimatize the student to common chord combinations, musical patterns, and song construction. As a result, the successful student of *Teach Yourself to Play Guitar* will have acquired a solid basis for advanced guitar instruction, musical composition, and songwriting.

To get the most out of this book—without curbing your enthusiasm!—take your time and read any accompanying text or performance suggestions carefully. It's also a good idea to review each completed (in other words, mastered) chapter before moving ahead. If extended guitar study is an eventual goal, the discipline built through the diligent practice and conscientious study of each lesson found within will be of great value to you. But even if all you want from this book is the means to a fun, pressure-free, and creative new hobby, the time you devote to each lesson will be repaid in greater accuracy, technique, and confidence.

Table of Contents

Chapter 1: Getting Started 4
Guitar anatomy, fingerboard diagrams, pitch, hand and finger placement,
picking and strumming, posture and position, tuning

Chapter 2: How to Read and Interpret the Notation Used in This Book 10
Chord diagrams, tablature, rhythm notation

Chapter 3: Open-Position Chords: Major Scale 14
G chord (1), G chord (2), C chord, D chord
    Song 1: *Amazing Grace* 18
    Song 2: *Home on the Range* 19

Chapter 4: Open-Position Chords: Minor Scale 20
Am chord, Em chord, Dm chord
    Song 3: *The Strumming Song* 24
    Song 4: *When Johnny Comes Marching Home* 25

Chapter 5: Power Chords 26
Basic power chords, power chord boogie
    Song 5: *12-Bar Blues Progression* 31
    Song 6: *AC/DC-Style Rock Progression* 31

Chapter 6: Single-Note Patterns 32
Major, minor, and combined single-note patterns
    Song 7: *Extended Single-Note Riff 1* 36
    Song 8: *Extended Single-Note Riff 2* 37

Chapter 7: Open-Position Scales 38
Major, minor, and pentatonic scales in open-position
    Song 9: *Auld Lang Syne* 41
    Song 10: *The Sailor's Hornpipe (Popeye's Theme)* 41

Chapter 8: Barre Chords 42
Open-position, 5-string, and full barre chords, major/minor barre chord comparisons
    Song 11: *Scarborough Fair* 46
    Song 12: *Canon in D* 47

Closing Note 47

Chapter 1
Getting Started

Guitar Anatomy

Let's start by going over the various components of your guitar, otherwise known as "guitar anatomy." The following illustrates the anatomy of both an electric and an acoustic guitar.

Although your guitar may have a different shape or look than the electric or acoustic guitars pictured below, its parts should be essentially the same.

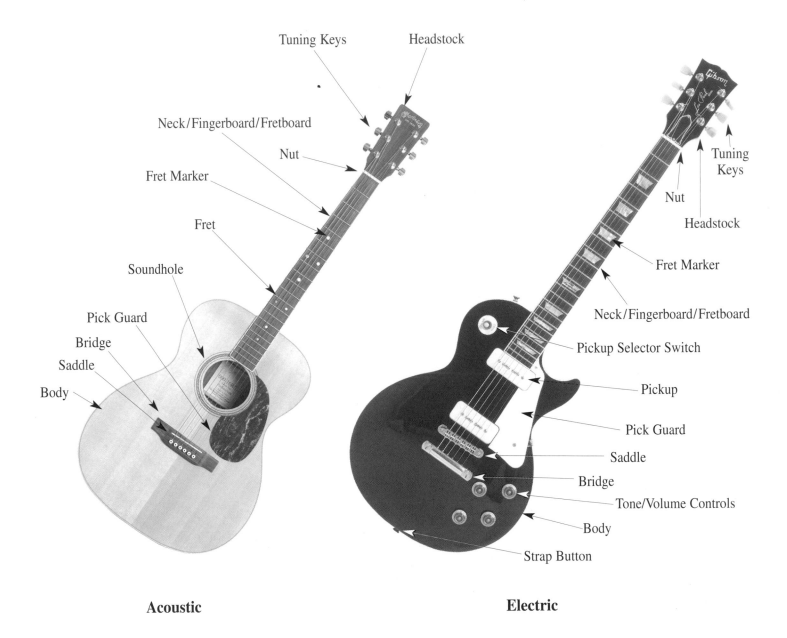

Acoustic   **Electric**

Notice that both the acoustic and electric guitar have many parts in common; however, some components are unique to each. Make sure that you're familiar with the names of all your guitar's components, as there will be occasional references to them throughout this book.

Fingerboard Diagrams

Take another look at your guitar's fingerboard. Notice the horizontal divisions that run its entire length. These divisions are the *frets*. Frets are numbered from 1–22 and run from "low" on the neck (just under the nut), to "high" (where the neck joins the body). We will depict sections of frets throughout this book by way of *fingerboard diagrams*; an example of which is shown below:

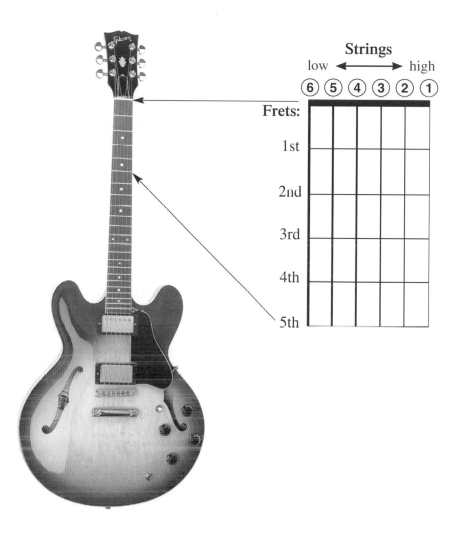

The vertical lines featured on the fingerboard diagrams represent the individual strings, which, left to right, are ordered from the thickest and lowest-sounding string, to the thinnest and highest-sounding string.

To indicate which fingers are used to play single notes or chords, some of the examples in this book refer to the fingers of your left hand by number, as shown below:

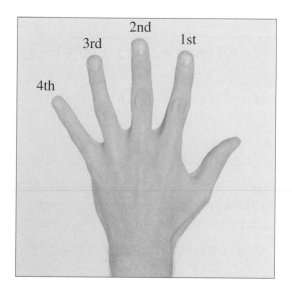

Pitch

As mentioned in the previous section, the guitar's strings are ordered from the lowest-sounding string to the highest. These differences in lowness and highness are called *pitch*. Each string is tuned to a particular pitch when *open* (not pressed or fretted). These pitches in order from lowest to highest are E–A–D–G–B–E. Strike each string in turn and notice the different sounds between each.

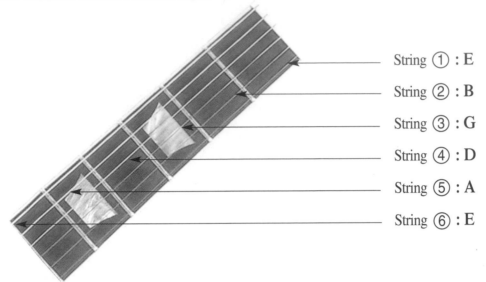

String ① : E

String ② : B

String ③ : G

String ④ : D

String ⑤ : A

String ⑥ : E

In addition, different pitches are also produced when the strings are depressed at different frets: when a string is depressed at the frets located "lower" on the neck (near the nut), the sound produced is lower; if the same string is pressed at the frets located "higher" on the neck (toward the bridge), the sound produced is higher. This will be discussed in more detail in Chapter 2.

Hand and Finger Placement

Like accurate tuning, proper hand and finger placement is crucial to effective playing. The photos below illustrate correct fret-hand placement:

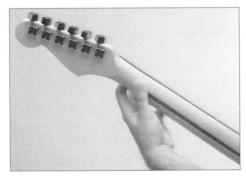

Place your thumb on the underside of the guitar neck.

Arch your fingers so that you will be able to reach all the strings more easily.

Avoid letting the palm of your hand touch the neck of the guitar.

It's crucial to a fretted note's or chord's sound production that you press the string correctly and in the proper place.

- If you apply too much of your fingertip's surface to the string, you could mute or dull the string's sound. Make sure that only the uppermost part of your finger (where it starts to curve toward the top) is used to apply pressure to the string.
- If you bend the string toward or away from it's placement in the center of the fret, you'll warp the sound. Make sure that you're applying pressure directly and firmly onto the string, so that it is less likely to slip forwards or backwards.
- If you place your finger on or too close to the metal fret, you will get a dull or buzzing sound from the struck string. Make sure that you're pressing down on the string closer to the middle of the fret.

Also, make sure that your fret hand is relaxed and not gripping the neck or pressing any strings too hard, or the note will sound sharp.

Picking and Strumming

To strike the strings, you will usually use a pick. The correct way to hold a pick is by gripping it between your thumb and index finger while keeping the rest of your hand relaxed and your fingers curved. Rest those fingers not holding the pick against the guitar for extra support.

You can either *pick* each string one at a time, or *strum* several of them together. To start, we'll be using a downward motion called the *downstroke*. Try strumming several strings at once with gentle and even downstrokes. Practice this several times to get the feel of the pick against the strings. Strike with enough force to create a solid and steady sound but not so hard that your pick bends or gets caught between the strings. Now try picking each string, one at a time, from bottom to top. Do this also until it starts to feel and sound both natural and easy. Then, reverse your picking direction to produce an *upstroke*, or upward striking motion.

Downstrokes will be notated on the exercises throughout with a downward-pointing arrow located beneath each corresponding note. Likewise, upstrokes will be indicated with an upward-pointing arrow:

Downstroke   *Upstroke*

Posture and Position

Posture should also be considered. Sitting is probably the most comfortable and least fatiguing way to play, at least at first. But if you prefer to stand, go for it! Whichever you choose, be mindful of the following guidelines:

- Balance your weight evenly from left to right, sit up straight, and position your body, arms, and legs so that they're tension-free.

- If you start to feel tension in any part of your body, that's probably an indication that you need to readjust your posture and position.

- Tilt the guitar's neck upwards—never downwards.

- Avoid the temptation to slant the topside of the guitar up and towards you to see the fretboard better. The goal is to finger the fretboard without looking at it—which you will soon be able to do with a little practice!

Tuning

In order to adjust the pitch (highness or lowness of sound) of your strings, you may need to tighten or loosen them at the tuning pegs. The diagram below shows which strings correspond to which tuning pegs:

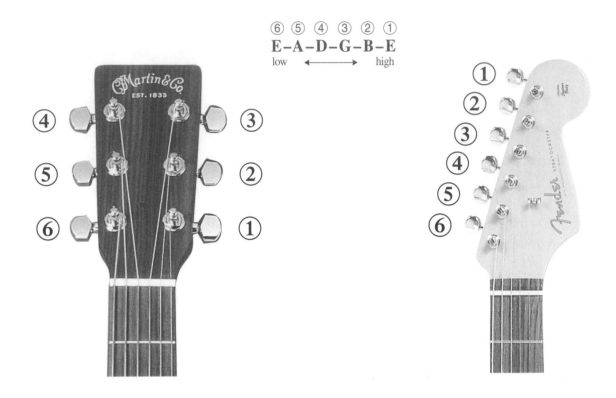

The process of adjusting the strings at the pegs for pitch is called tuning. You have a couple of different options for tuning your guitar:

Electronic Tuner

Until you've become familiar with correct pitch, an electronic tuner may be your most reliable tuning option. These tuners "read" the pitch produced from a plucked open string and indicate on a meter whether the pitch is correct, flat, or sharp. Using the tuning keys, you then either tighten or loosen the string until the meter indicates that the pitch is correct.

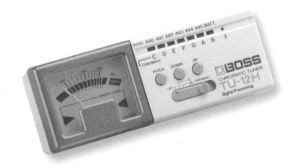

Piano/Keyboard

If you have a tuned piano or keyboard at your disposal, and know where "middle C" is located, you can tune each guitar string by ear according to the sound of the corresponding piano/keyboard note. Although tweaking your strings' pitches this way may seem a bit daunting at first, this is a good way to practice hearing pitch.

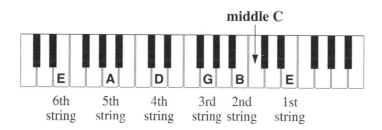

Relative Tuning

Another way to tune your guitar by ear is to do so in relation to your guitar's other strings. The following diagram illustrates how to tune by this method:

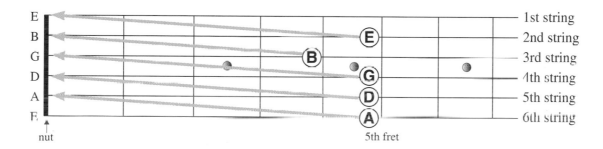

1. Tune the 6th string E to a piano, a pitch pipe, or an electronic tuner.
   If none of these are available, approximate E as best you can.
2. Press the 6th string at the 5th fret. This is A. Tune the open 5th string to this pitch.
3. Press the 5th string at the 5th fret. This is D. Tune the open 4th string to this pitch.
4. Press the 4th string at the 5th fret. This is G. Tune the open 3rd string to this pitch.
5. Press the 3rd string at the 4th fret. This is B. Tune the open 2nd string to this pitch.
6. Press the 2nd string at the 5th fret. This is E. Tune the open 1st string to this pitch.

Some things to consider when using the relative tuning or keyboard/piano methods:

- Always turn the peg slowly (whether tightening or loosening the string) so that you can clearly discern the change in pitch that results from this adjustment. You may also need to pluck and adjust the string repeatedly before getting the correct pitch.

- Listen for a series of pulsating *beat waves;* these indicate how far or close to correct pitch you are. The farther you are from correct pitch, the faster the beat waves; the closer you are to correct pitch, the slower the beat waves. When the beat waves stop completely, you're at correct pitch.

- Always tune a string up instead of down. Begin by tuning your string below the desired pitch, and then slowly tune up until correct pitch is achieved. Doing so will stretch the string into place, which will help it stay in tune longer.

Chapter 2
How to Read and Interpret the Notation Used in This Book

This book is designed to teach guitar to those students with little or no music-reading experience; therefore, standard music notation will neither be used nor taught here. But for instructional purposes, some form of notation is necessary. The following sections discuss the chord diagrams, tablature, and rhythm notation that will be used throughout this book.

Chord Diagrams

The first style of notation you should become familiar with is called a chord diagram. The vertical lines of the chord diagram represent the guitar's strings, and the horizontal lines represent its frets:

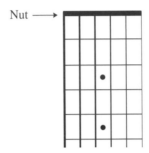

In the chord diagrams used throughout this book, where you place your fingers to form a particular chord is depicted by black dots placed on the appropriate frets and strings:

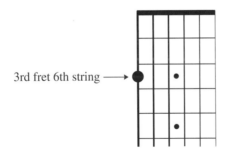

The correct fingers used to form a chord are indicated by numbers along the bottom of the diagram. For example, the chord frame below illustrates a C major chord formed with the 3rd finger on the 3rd fret of the 5th string, the 2nd finger on the 2nd fret of the 4th string, and the 1st finger on the 1st fret of the 2nd string. Additionally, the "X" above the 6th string indicates that string should be *muted*. And the "O" symbols above the 3rd and 1st strings indicate those strings should be played open:

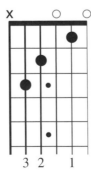

10

Tablature

Tablature, or "tab" for short, has been around for years but has recently gained more popularity and acceptance as an alternative to standard music notation. It is now a commonly used feature in guitar magazines, instructional and transcription books, and guitar-related websites.

The structure of tab is quite simple: the six lines of the tab staff represent the six strings of the guitar (like the chord diagram, only horizontally oriented), in the order shown below:

Strings to be played "open" are indicated with a zero (0) placed on the appropriate string:

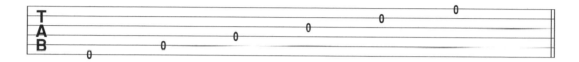

Muted strings are depicted on the appropriate string using an X:

Tab for Single Notes

Tab is used to indicate both single notes and chords. The fret to be pressed to play a single note is indicated by a number placed on a particular string. A series of these numbers is read from left to right. Once the first note indicated has been struck, it can be released and the next note in the series played.

The example below shows a pattern of single notes in tab notation. It begins with the 3rd fret of the 6th string, and then proceeds to an open 4th string, an open 3rd string, and then back to the open 4th string. Then, the melodic pattern is repeated:

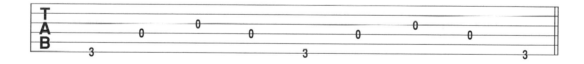

Here is an exercise to help you become more familiar with reading tab for single notes. Note the downward-pointing arrows, which indicate that a downstroke should be used when picking:

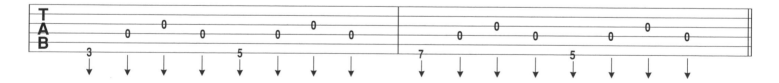

> *The pattern illustrated above is called an* arpeggio, *which occurs when the notes of a chord are played individually and separately. This is a very popular technique used in all styles of music, so be sure to spend some time playing these arpeggio patterns before moving ahead in this book.*

Tab for Chords

Tab notation indicates that a chord is to be played when the fret numbers are stacked in a vertical line. To form the chord shown below, place your 2nd finger on the 3rd fret of the 6th string, your 1st finger on the 2nd fret of the 5th string, and your 3rd finger on the 3rd fret of the 1st string. The 4th, 3rd, and 2nd strings are all struck as open strings (indicated by the "0s").

Play the chords with downstrokes in series of four, to familiarize yourself with reading tab for chords:

Rhythm Notation

Now that you're familiar with tab for both single notes and chords, and recognize the downstroke and upstroke notation, let's move on to rhythm notation. With *standard notation*, rhythm is indicated by symbols that represent the length of time that either a *note* should be sounded or that a *rest* should be held silent. Because this book is for the student with no music-reading knowledge, standard notation will not be used. However, because rhythm is a crucial element in music, some form of notation must be employed to indicate this. That rhythm convention is *tab rhythm notation*, which is widely used and accepted today.

The figure below is tab that has been broken up into sections by vertical lines; these sections are called *measures*. The double line at the end of the tab indicates the end of the final measure. The duration of each measure is specified by the *time signature*, which is found at the beginning of a musical piece:

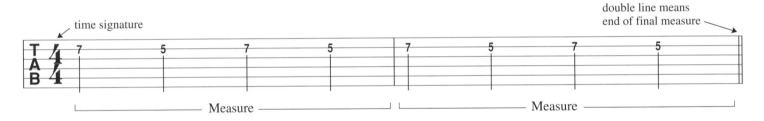

The time signature is notated as a fraction; the bottom numeral indicates the note value of the rhythm pattern, and the top numeral indicates the number of beats that make up the pattern. For example, tab marked with a 4/4 time signature will have four quarter-note (1/4) beats per measure; a 3/4 time signature will have three quarter-note (1/4) beats per measure.

The tab notation within each measure also includes the appropriate rhythm markers, which indicate the number of beats that each note or chord receives. The example below shows the beat values for the various rhythm markers when the time signature features a "4" as the denominator (4/4, 3/4, 2/4):

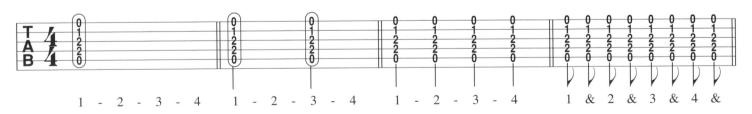

| Whole-beat marker: 4 counts | Half-beat marker: 2 counts | Quarter-beat marker: 1 count | Eighth-beat marker: 1/2 count |

The stems of rhythm markers may point upwards or downwards, depending on their placement on the tab staff; however, the direction of the stem has no effect on the value of the beat.

Sometimes a series of eighth notes will be joined at their stems by a *beam*. These are counted "1 and 2 and 3 and 4 and." Three eighth notes beamed in a single beat are called *triplets,* which are counted "1-uh-let, 2-uh-let, etc."

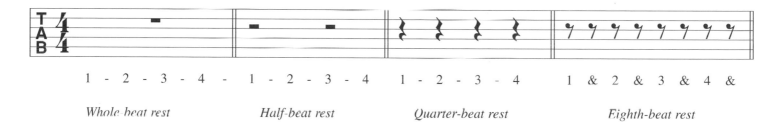

Beamed eighth notes   *Beamed eighth-note triplets*

There are also rhythm markers to indicate instances when no music is played or held, but that there should be a silence for a specified length of time. These markers are called *rests*:

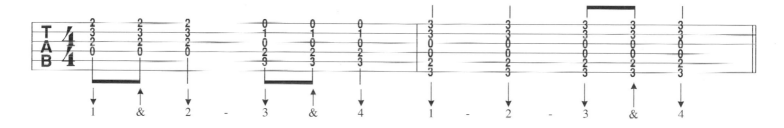

Whole-beat rest   *Half-beat rest*   *Quarter-beat rest*   *Eighth-beat rest*

Use the following three exercises to become more familiar with the rhythm notation used in this book:

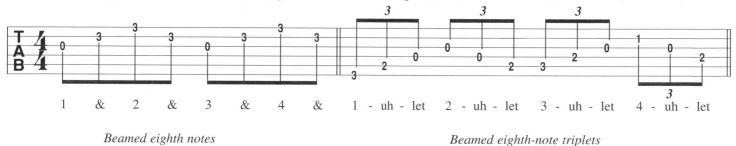

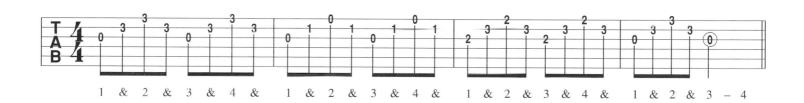

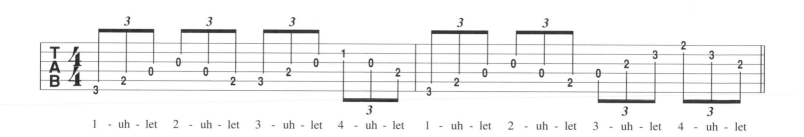

Chapter 3
Open-Position Chords: Major Scale

Open-position chords are considered the most basic. They are played lower on the neck (near the nut) and often include open strings. Used by both acoustic and electric guitarists, open-position chords are featured in every musical style—especially rock, jazz, blues, folk, classical, and country. The chords featured in this chapter are the most common and can be found in a multitude of songs.

Major chords are those that belong to the major scale; their sound could be described as positive, bright, or happy.

G Chord (Version 1)

Let's start with the very common open-position G major chord:

Using the chord diagram as your guide, place your 1st finger on the 2nd fret of the 5th string, your 2nd finger on the 3rd fret of the 6th string, and your 3rd finger on the 3rd fret of the 1st string. Make sure your fingers are pressing the strings firmly and solidly, but keep your hand and wrist relaxed.

> *To ensure that you are forming the chord properly and sounding all of the notes correctly, play it as an arpeggio (the notes struck individually and in sequence), and listen to each string of the chord as it is plucked. Do you hear any dull or buzzing sound when a particular string is struck? If so, you may be pressing the string with too much of your fingertip, or your hand is inadvertently touching the strings. Reposition your fingers and press the strings firmly to help correct any problems.*

Next, strum the strings using downstrokes. You can also slightly vary the sound by strumming with upstrokes. Notice also the rhythm notation (steady and consistent quarter-note beats) and play accordingly:

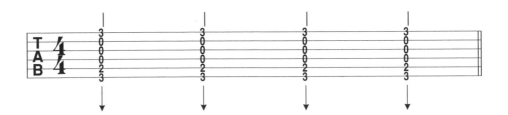

G Chord (Version 2)

Now that you are familiar with playing the G major chord, try an alternative version of this chord. The second version of this chord is fingered in almost the same manner as the first; the only difference is the inclusion of the 3rd fret on the B string (note the finger numbers on the chord diagram):

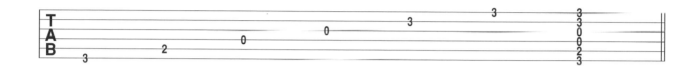

Now try this strumming exercise to get familiar with this alternative G major chord:

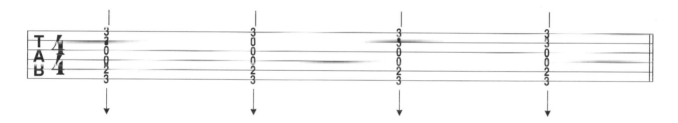

C Chord

The next open-position chord to learn is the C major chord, which is also a very common chord in all styles of music. Notice that with this open chord, only five of the guitar's six strings are involved, so be careful not to sound or pick the 6th string (the low E) when performing this chord:

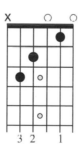

Begin by playing the individual notes of the C major chord as an arpeggio, and then form the chord and strum the strings with a downstroke.

Once you feel you're comfortable with the C chord, strum through the following exercise:

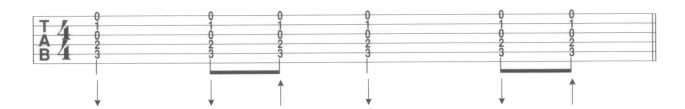

This exercise introduces a rhythm different from those of the previous examples. A pair of eighth-note strums follows each quarter-note strum. Practice this rhythm, playing it as steadily yet as musically as possible.

G–C Chord Progression

Now that you're more comfortable with the C major chord shape, let's try switching between it and a G major chord. This combination, or *progression*, is very common and featured in countless songs:

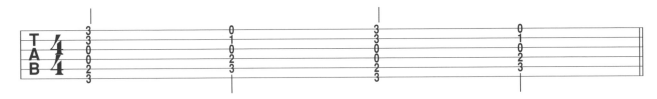

The next exercise features the same progression, but incorporates the alternating quarter-note to eighth-note rhythm introduced above. Take care to play this piece evenly and melodically:

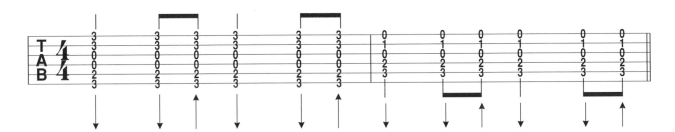

Not all music is in 4/4 time. Sometimes, there are only *three* beats per measure. This is called 3/4 time and is counted "one, two, three." This also introduces a new rhythm marker: the dotted half note. A dot adds one half of the preceding note's rhythmic value, so a dot next to a half note indicates a rhythmic duration of three beats:

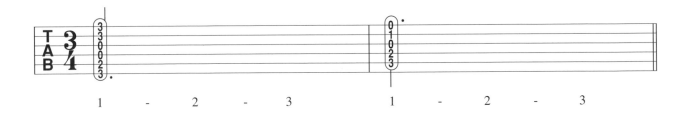

D Chord

D major is another common open-position chord that has been used in every style of music. Notice that you are using only four of the six strings of the guitar with the D chord. Be sure not to sound the E or A strings when performing this chord:

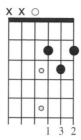

Play the D major chord as an arpeggio, and then strum the strings with a downstroke.

Once you're comfortable with playing the above, practice the D major chord with this strumming exercise:

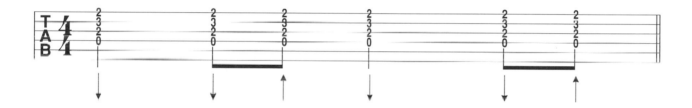

G–C–D Chord Progression

Now let's play these three chords together. The G–C–D chord progression is common to all styles of music—especially folk, country, blues, and '80s power ballads.

To practice switching between these chords, try strumming this progression:

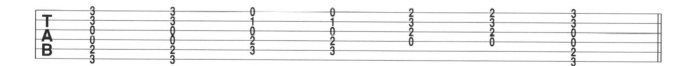

Don't get discouraged if this sequence of chords seems hard to execute at first. Continue to practice moving your fingers from one chord to the other and forming each chord shape. The transition between chords should be as smooth as possible, so that you get a connected, flowing sound.

When you're comfortable making these transitions, try this strumming exercise. Be mindful of the rhythm pattern!

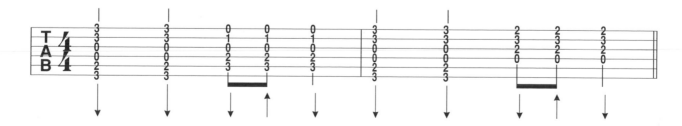

Song 1: Amazing Grace

Once you are comfortable playing the four chords covered in Chapter 3, you're ready to put your hard work to use. "Amazing Grace" features the G, C, and D chords. Notice that this song is in 3/4 time. This means there are three quarter-note beats per measure. To strum along, strum a downstroke on each beat.

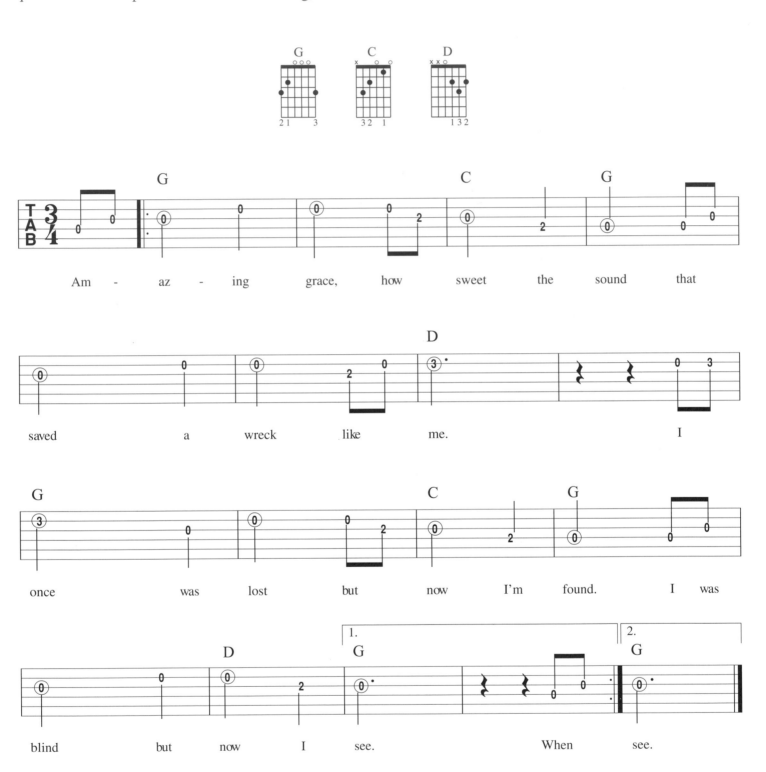

Song 2: Home on the Range

As mentioned before, there are countless popular songs that use the G, C, and D chords, and another example is the timeless American folk song, "Home on the Range." Note here that instead of the D major, this song features a "D5." Just follow the chord diagram below to form this easy-to-execute chord.

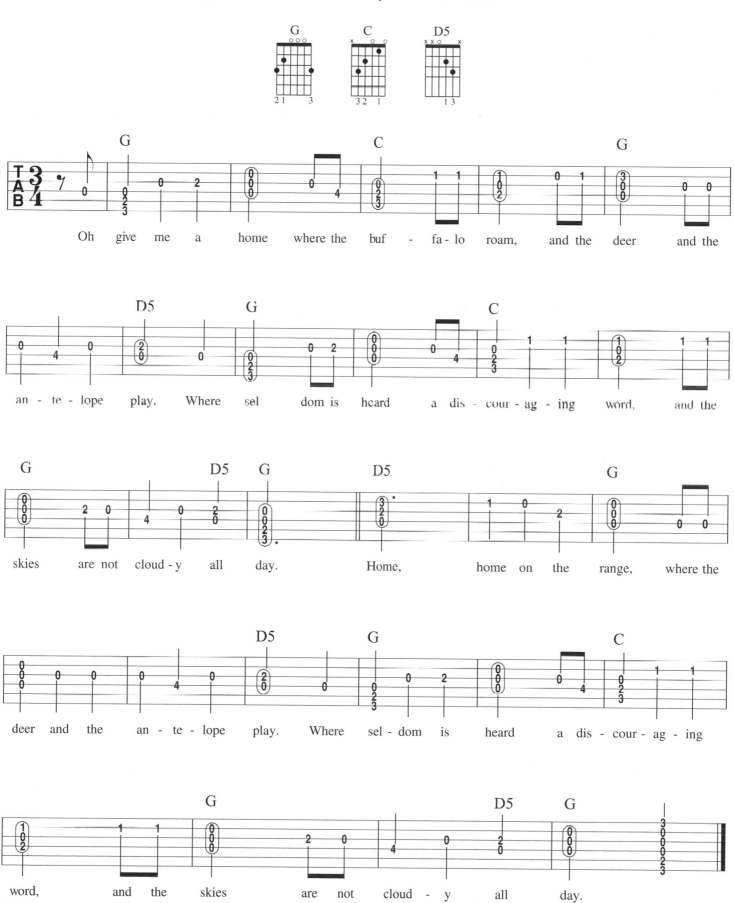

Chapter 4
Open-Position Chords: Minor Scale

Continuing with open-position chords, we'll now introduce a few that belong to the minor scale. With a tonal quality opposite that of the major chords, minor chords could be described as having a dark, or melancholy sound.

Am Chord

Let's start with one of the more popular of the open-position minor chords, the A minor:

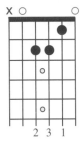

Play the A minor chord as an arpeggio, and then strum the strings with a downstroke.

Now play through the following strumming exercise, paying close attention to the rhythm pattern:

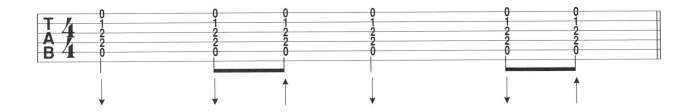

Am–D–G Chord Progression

Major/minor chord combinations have an interesting and pleasing tonality. The next example incorporates the A minor chord with the D and G major chords. Note again the particular rhythm pattern:

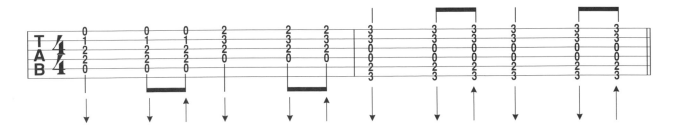

This example reverses the progression, thus creating a completely different tonal "flavor:"

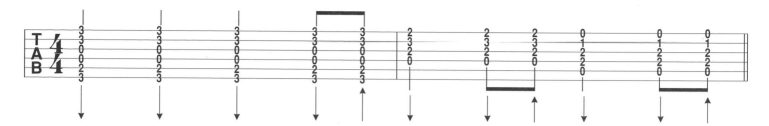

C–Am–D–G Chord Progression

The following exercise includes the C major chord, thus creating a four-chord pattern. Take your time to get the chord transitions smooth:

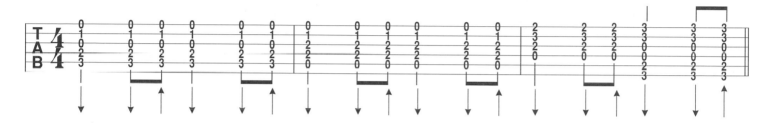

Am /A Comparison

For every major chord there is a minor chord equivalent. The examples below illustrate how to convert the A minor chord to an A major:

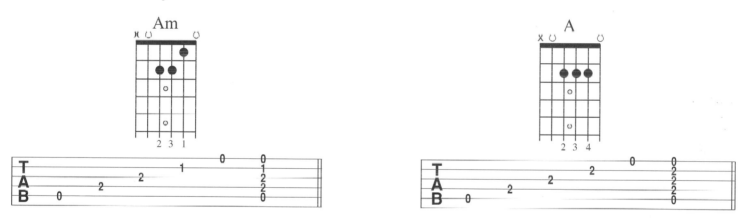

Play the A minor and A major chords as arpeggios, and then strum.

Em Chord

Next, let's learn an open-position E minor chord:

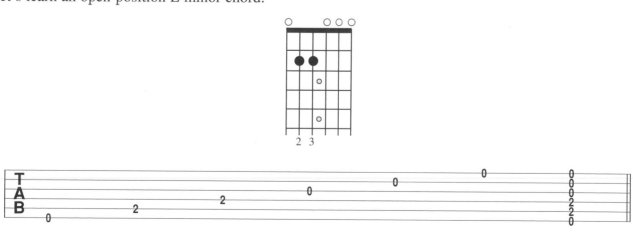

Play the E minor chord as an arpeggio, and then strum the strings with a downstroke.

21

Now, try strumming the exercise below. Notice the rhythm notation and play accordingly:

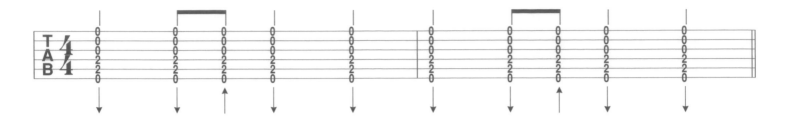

Em–Am Chord Progression

The following example incorporates both of the minor chords you've learned so far:

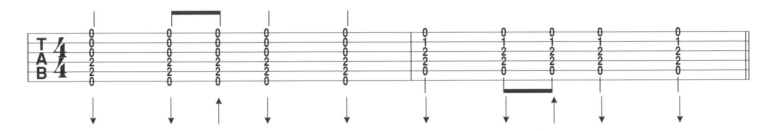

G–Em–Am–D Chord Progression

Now play the popular chord progression shown here:

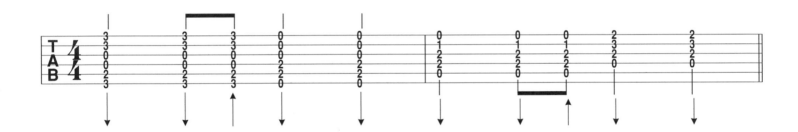

Em /E Comparison

Follow the chord diagrams to transform the E minor chord to an E major chord:

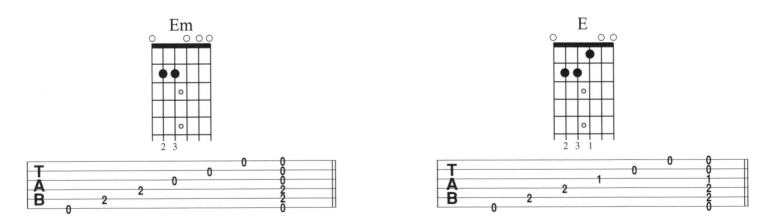

Follow the tab and play the E minor and E major chords as arpeggios. Then, strum each chord.

Dm Chord

Now try the open-position D minor chord:

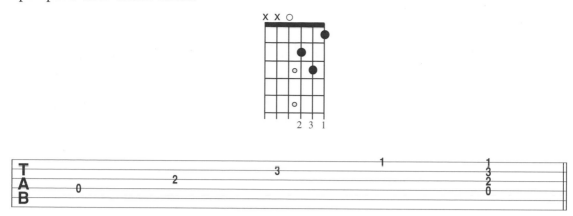

Play the D minor chord as an arpeggio, and then strum it. Next, play the following strumming exercise. Notice the rhythm notation and play accordingly:

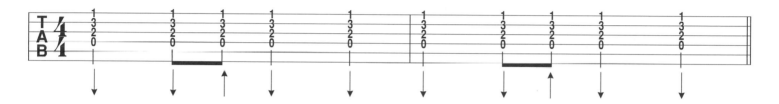

Dm–Em–Am Chord Progression

Once you're comfortable playing the D minor chord, practice the chord progression below:

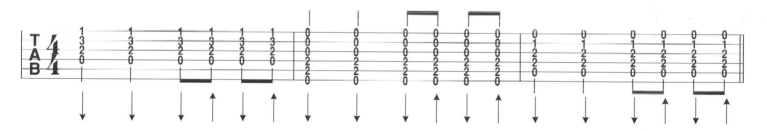

Dm / D Comparison

Follow the chord diagrams to transform the D minor chord to a D major chord:

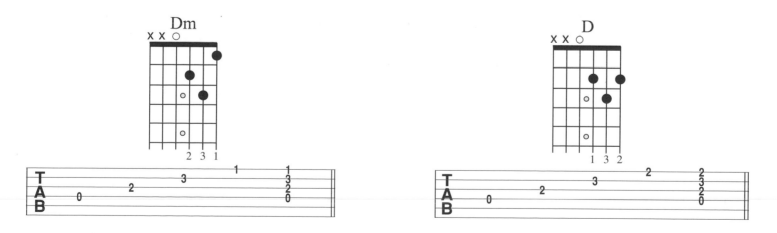

Play the D minor and D major chords as arpeggios, and then strum each chord.

The major and minor chords covered in Chapters 3 and 4 are just a few of several (others will be covered in the chapter on barre chords). Your job at this point is to take the time now to review the exercises from these two chapters to make sure that you can properly perform all of the chords and strumming patterns that you've learned so far.

Song 3: The Strumming Song

"The Strumming Song" incorporates four of the chords you've learned so far: Dm, Am, Em, and C. Pay close attention to the rhythm notation.

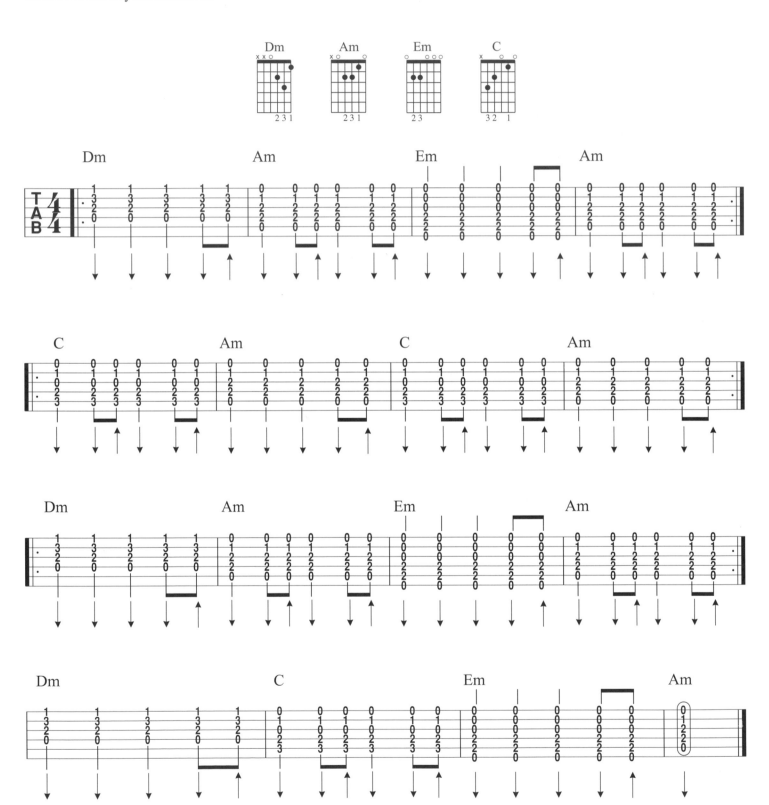

Song 4: When Johnny Comes Marching Home

Here's a well-known song that features the three minor chords and two of the major chords that you've learned so far. Pay close attention to the rhythm notation.

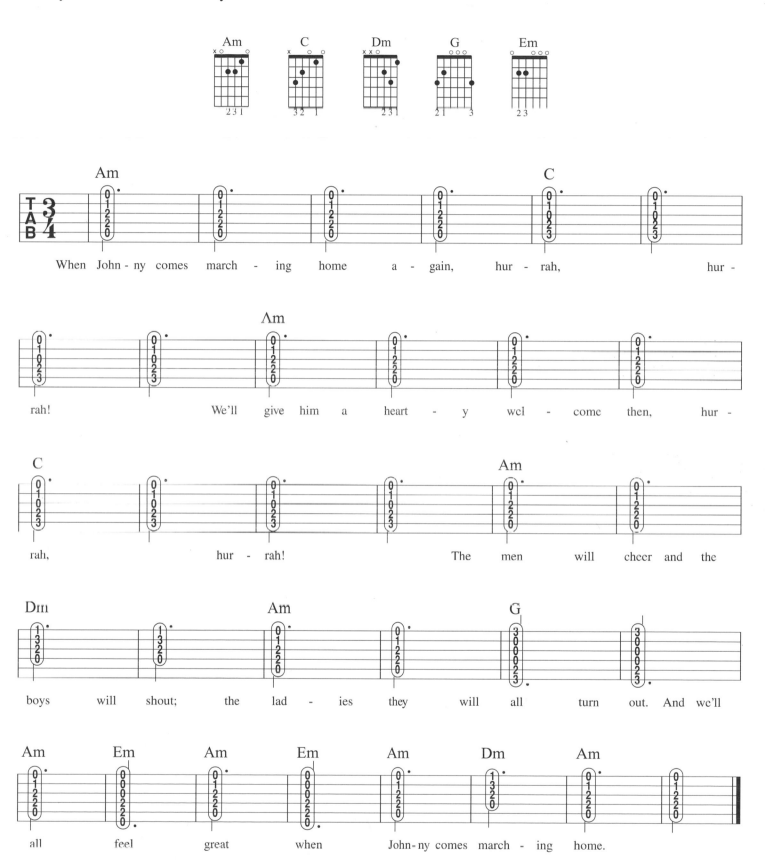

Chapter 5
Power Chords

Power chords—even though they consist of only two notes—sound "powerful," and most guitarists incorporate them into their playing at one time or another. Power chords are composed of a root note (name of the chord) and the 5th scale degree. As such they are also know as "5" chords. These chords' lack of complexity makes them un-cluttered and efficient choices for all sorts of ensemble playing, especially when performing with a keyboardist.

E5 Chord

Take a look at the chord diagram and the tab of the E5 power chord:

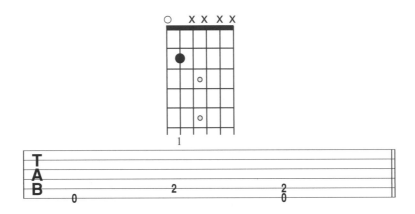

Start by picking the open 6th string (low E string) and fretted 5th string separately. Once you've played them sepa-rately, sound the notes together as a strummed chord. Make absolutely certain that you're striking only those two strings together without sounding the remaining four.

Play through the picking exercise below to make sure that you're sounding the E5 power chord correctly:

One technique often used in conjunction with power chords is palm-muting. *This involves lightly resting the "blade" side of your picking hand against the strings, near the bridge. Palm-muting results in a "chunky" attack commonly heard in rock music.*

Play the next example using all downstrokes. In the first measure, play normally; in the second measure, use palm-muting (P.M.), and listen carefully to the different effect this has on the sound:

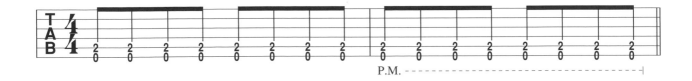

A5 Chord

Moving from the E5 power chord shape to the A5 power chord shape is simple to do in open position: Simply move your 1st finger from the 2nd fret on the 5th string to the 2nd fret on the 4th string. You now have an open-position A5 power chord:

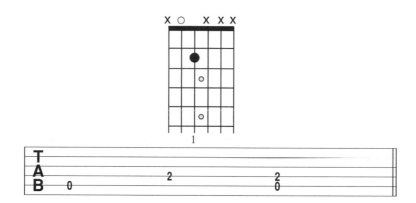

Now try the following picking exercise, making sure you're paying attention to the rhythm notation:

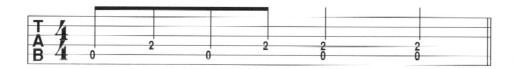

D5 Chord

Now move your 1st finger to the 2nd fret on the 3rd string and sound it along with the open 4th string. This is the D5 power chord:

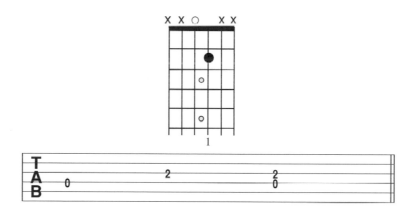

Play through this picking exercise to learn the D5 power chord. Watch for the palm-mute:

G5 Chord

Let's continue shifting across the strings. Position your 1st finger on the 3rd fret of the 2nd string while playing the open 3rd string. This creates an open-position G5 power chord:

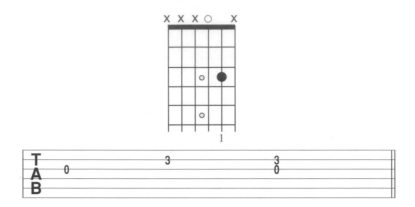

Now play the picking exercise below. Notice the rhythm variation featured here; this separates the sound of this example from the previous ones:

B5 Chord

The final power chord involves moving to the 2nd fret on the 1st string and playing it with the open 2nd string. This creates an open-position B5 power chord:

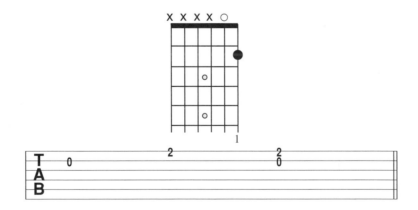

Play through the following picking exercise, making sure to pay attention to the rhythm notation:

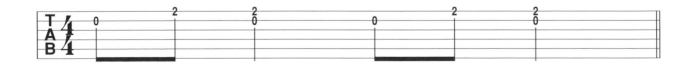

Now let's put some of these power chords to use. The following exercise uses power chords in arpeggio form, strummed, and palm-muted. Take your time to learn the big shifts in rhythm:

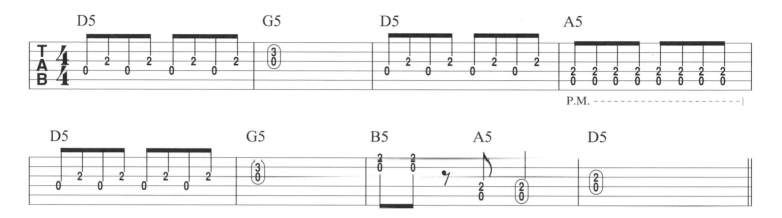

Power Chord Boogie

Once you have played through all of the previous power chord shapes, you should be ready to tackle the power chord boogie—which means alternating between power chords in a boogie rhythm.

A5–A6 Shift

The example below illustrates the A5–A6 power chord shift, which can be found in blues, rock, and even country songs. To begin, let's learn the fingering for a basic boogie pattern. First, play the A5 power chord in open position. Then move the fretted note from the 2nd fret to the 4th fret on the 4th string. This combination of the open A string and 4th fret creates a chord called a "6" chord, in this case, A6:

Now, to give this chord sequence a more authentic boogie flavor, play it with the doubled strum pattern notated below:

One popular form of the boogie sound involves the "shuffle" rhythm. The shuffle rhythm is created by playing the first of two consecutive eighth notes with a slightly longer duration than the second.

Now, go back and play the double-strummed A5-A6 example above, but this time, add a "shuffle" feel to it. And for even more blues flavor, add a slight palm mute as well.

D5–D6 Shift

Now that you're comfortable with the A5–A6 shift, let's move on to a shift in the key of D, as shown here:

Now apply a boogie rhythm pattern to the D5–D6 chord sequence:

E5–E6 Shift

The final chord shift is from E5 to E6:

Now, play through this exercise, again using the boogie rhythm:

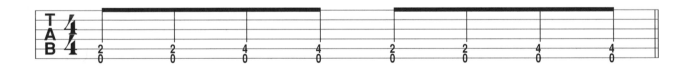

Try this boogie variation:

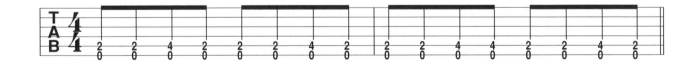

Song 5: 12-Bar Blues Progression

Now that you're comfortable with shifting power chords, give this "12-Bar Blues Progression" a try. It incorporates all three of the doubled rhythm riffs you learned in the previous section.

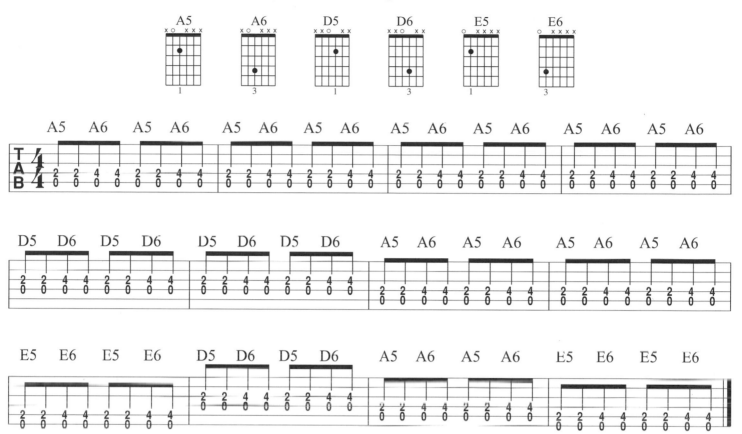

Song 6: AC/DC-Style Rock Progression

Power chords are as versatile as they are abundant. From the early blues pioneers to gritty rock bands like Led Zeppelin, many musicians have incorporated power chords into their signature sounds.

Play around with Song 6, which is a simplified version of the type of power-chord riff that rock bands such as AC/DC have employed to great use for decades. Notice that, since there is not much shift between power chords, the rhythm is critical to the song's sound, so take care to follow the rhythm notation exactly. NOTE: this song should be played "straight," that is, without a "shuffle" feel.

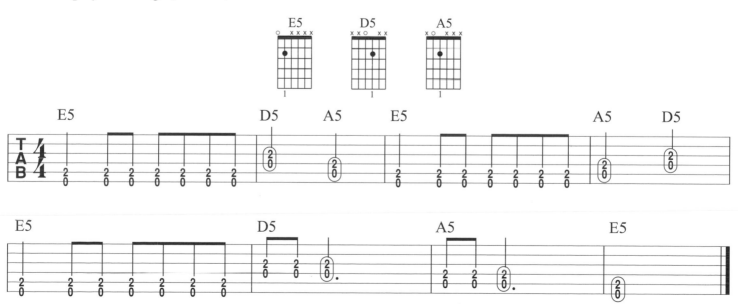

Chapter 6
Single-Note Patterns

The topics covered so far in this book have consisted of strumming patterns and arpeggiated picking exercises for both major and minor chords; but now that you're more comfortable with a variety of chord shapes, you're ready to learn *single-note patterns*—melody lines, riffs, and licks—which you can incorporate into and play in collaboration with strummed chord patterns.

Major Chord Single-Note Patterns

Let's start with some single-note patterns using the major chords covered in Chapter 3.

G Pattern

Let's start with a single-note pattern that involves the G major chord and an ascending two-note walk-up (a pattern that requires your fingers to move, or "walk," up the fingerboard), which starts on the open 6th string:

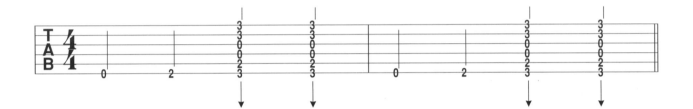

Now that you're familiar with a walk-up, let's try a walk-down (the note pattern descends the fingerboard). The next exercise combines the G major chord with a two-note walk-down pattern on the 5th string:

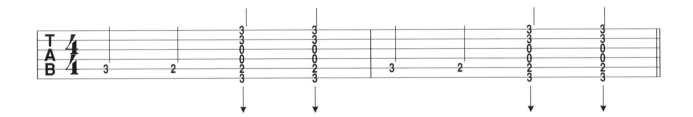

This next exercise combines both single-note patterns:

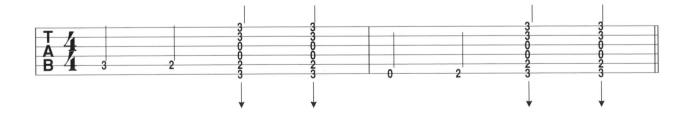

C Pattern

Once you are comfortable playing the G major single-note patterns, walk the ascending single notes to reach the open-position C major chord:

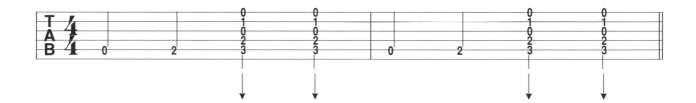

This next exercise features an ascending single-note triplet pattern with the C major chord. (To review the triplet rhythm, go back to p. 13.)

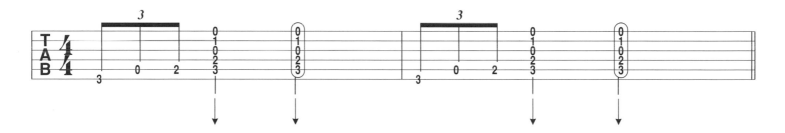

C–G Combined Single-Note Pattern

The following exercise combines two single-note moves using both the C and G major chords; this creates a melodic, cool-sounding riff:

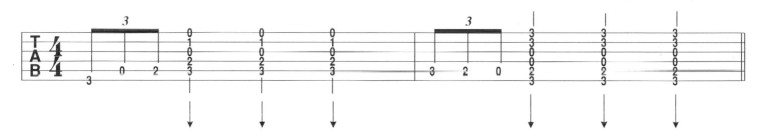

D Pattern

The next exercise features a descending, single-note triplet pattern with the D major chord in open position:

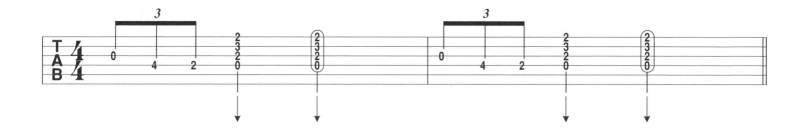

This exercise features another single-note triplet pattern with the D major chord. Keep in mind that the movement required to get from the single notes on the 5th string to the formation of the D major chord may be difficult to perform at first, but it will become much easier with practice:

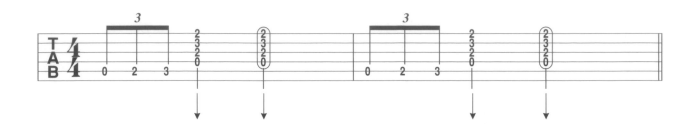

Minor Chord Single-Note Patterns

Now let's discuss some single-note patterns using the minor chords you learned in Chapter 4.

Am Pattern

This first exercise features a descending two-note pattern leading to an A minor chord:

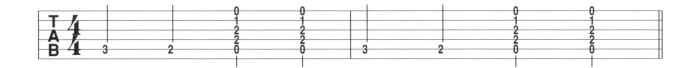

Now, play through the ascending triplet pattern with A minor:

Em Pattern

Let's move on to a single-note pattern using the E minor chord:

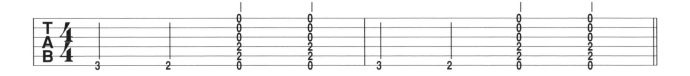

When you have mastered the descending two-note pattern in the previous exercise, try tackling the triplet pattern here:

Am–Em Combined Single-Note Pattern

Now combine the A minor and E minor chords together with single-note riffs:

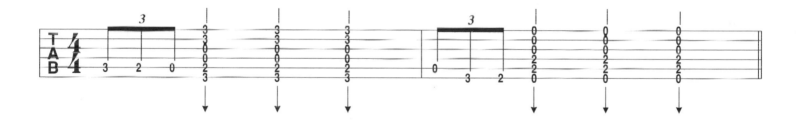

G–Em Combined Single-Note Pattern

This exercise connects a G major chord with an E minor chord by way of a three-note pattern played on the 5th and 6th strings:

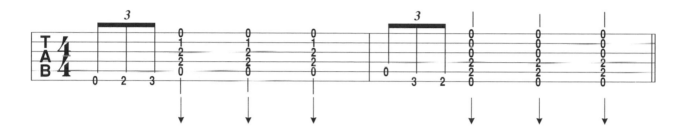

Am–C Combined Single-Note Pattern

Here is another three-note pattern, this time with A minor and C major chords:

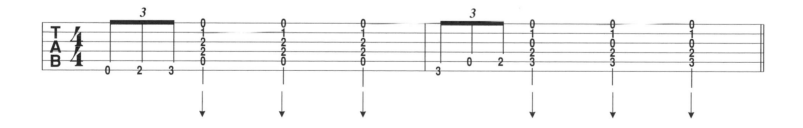

Song 7: Extended Single-Note Riff 1

Song 7 incorporates some of the single-note patterns covered in this chapter. Note that all of the single-note riffs are in triplet rhythms.

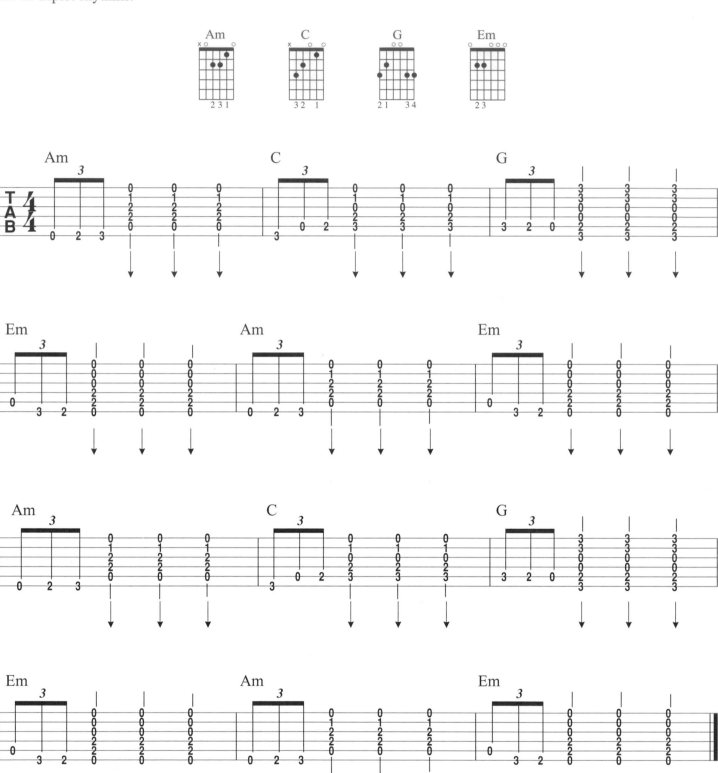

Song 8: Extended Single-Note Riff 2

Now play through Song 8, which incorporates the D major chord.

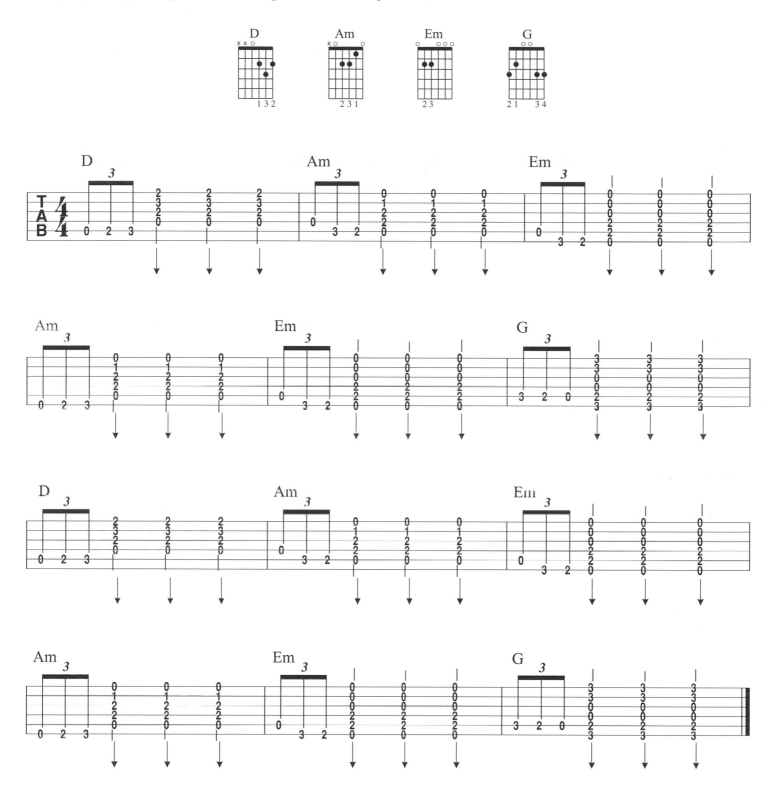

Chapter 7
Open-Position Scales

Learning *open-position scales* will help you become more familiar with the groupings of single notes arranged into different keys—a system of seven tones and harmonies arranged hierarchically. Scales are important, as they are the foundations of melodies, solos, fills, and riffs. In addition, learning and practicing them will improve your finger strength and dexterity.

Major Scales in Open Position

Each key includes major and minor scales. Let's start by covering some of the major scales.

C Scale

This example features the C major scale in open position:

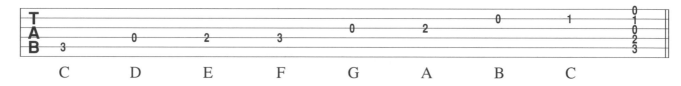

Now, play the scale again, and then strum the C chord to compare the notes of the C major scale to the sound of a C major chord. Notice the similarity in the tonality of each? That's because the notes that comprise a C major chord are from the C major scale.

To help you become more familiar with the C major scale, practice the popular "Lullaby" melody by classical composer Brahms illustrated below:

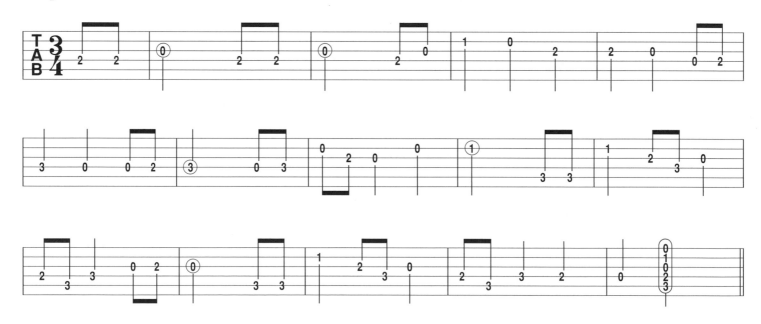

G Scale

Now try the G major scale:

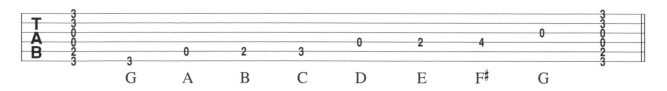

To become more familiar with the G major scale, here is Johann Sebastian Bach's popular melody, "Minuet in G:"

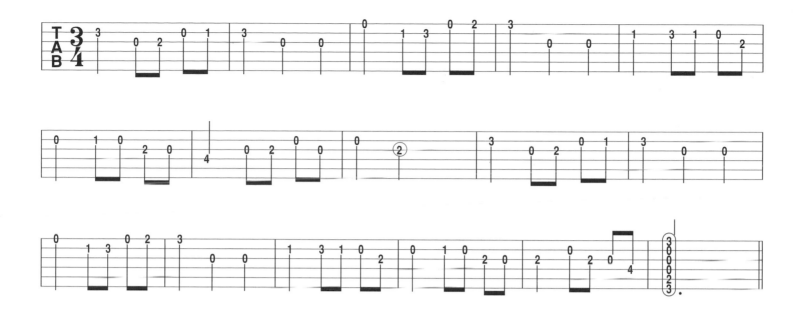

Minor Scales in Open Position

Am Scale

Now that you know a couple of the major scales, let's move on to the A minor scale, which is featured below. Ironically, this scale contains the same notes as the C major scale, but starting on A, instead of C:

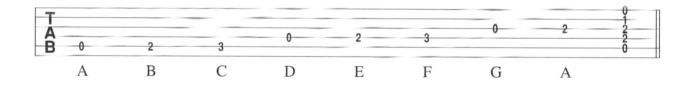

Now play the scale again, and then strum the chord to compare the notes of the A minor scale to the sound of an A minor chord.

Em Scale

Let's move on to the E minor scale in open position:

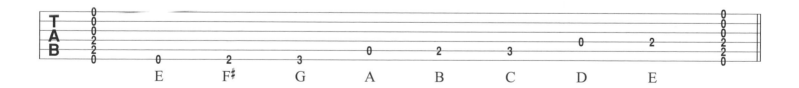

Pentatonic Scales in Open Position

Pentatonic scales—or five-note scales—are most common to musical styles such as blues, rock, country, and jazz.

Em Pentatonic Scale

The E minor pentatonic scale contains the notes E–G–A–B–D. It's an easy-to-fret, two-note-per-string open-position scale:

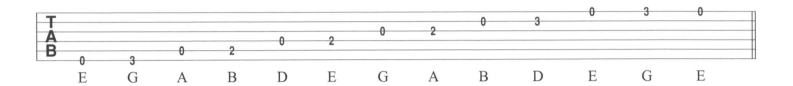

Using this pentatonic scale, try the basic blues lick below:

G Pentatonic Scale

Here is a G major pentatonic scale in open position. Play the scale followed by the chord to hear how they compare:

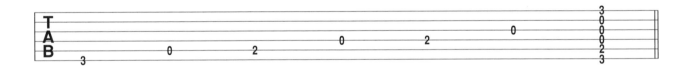

The notes of the G major pentatonic scale are the same as those of the E minor pentatonic scale; the difference between the two being the note of emphasis. In other words, with the G major pentatonic scale, the starting and ending notes are G, whereas with the E minor pentatonic scale, the home, or strongest note, is E.

Now that you're familiar with pentatonic scales, create some pentatonic patterns of your own. Just group various notes from a particular scale together to create melodic patterns and musical sequences. Pentatonic scales are considered the "guitarist's scale," because it's used by so many famous guitarists—B.B. King, Eric Clapton, Jimi Hendrix, and Eddie Van Halen, just to name a few.

Song 9: Auld Lang Syne

Song 8, the popular New Year's theme "Auld Lang Syne," incorporates some of the scales covered in this chapter.

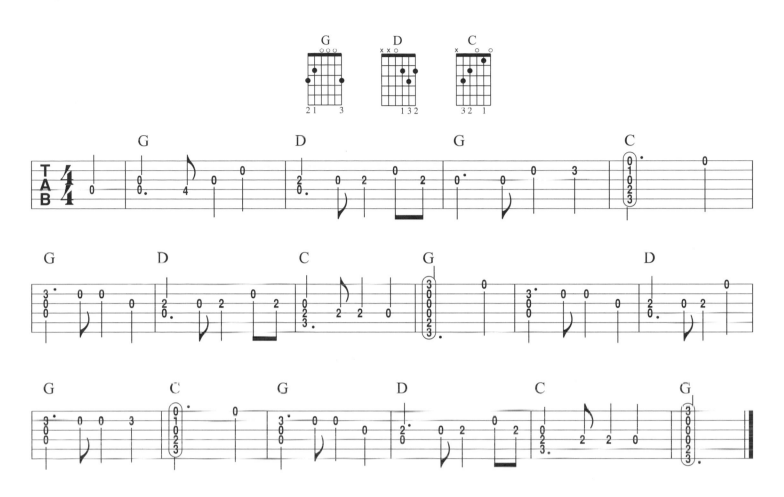

Song 10: The Sailor's Hornpipe (Popeye's Theme)

Now try this recognizable tune, "The Sailor's Hornpipe," which is more commonly known as "Popeye's Theme."

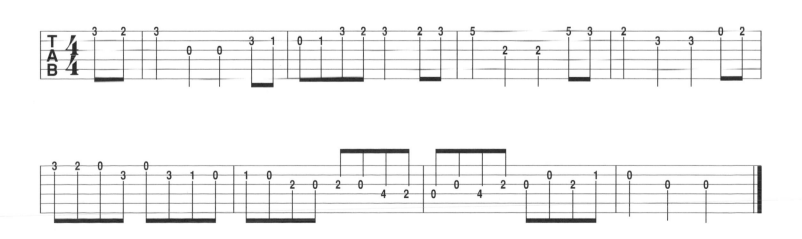

Chapter 8
Barre Chords

Barre chords are common to every style of music. However, to many beginning guitarists, they are somewhat difficult to execute. But it gets easier when you learn that the trick to performing barre chords is simply to apply just the right amount of pressure to the strings.

Open-Position Barre Chords

F Barre Chord

The first barre chord to tackle is the open-position F major chord:

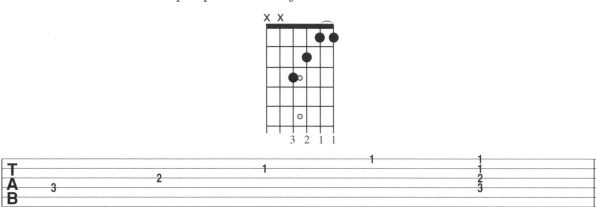

Once you're able to perform this chord correctly and accurately, try the next exercise, which incorporates it into a progression featuring some of the open-position chords you've already learned:

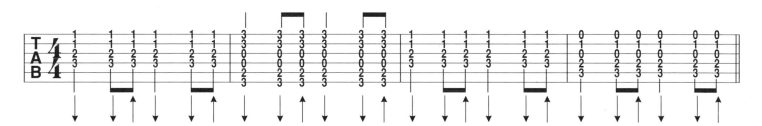

The F major barre chord shape can be moved around the fretboard to create different chords. The next exercise demonstrates a shift to G major:

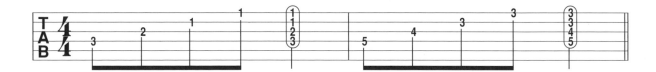

This exercise features the same progression as before, but here the G major chord is played as a barre chord instead of as an open-position chord:

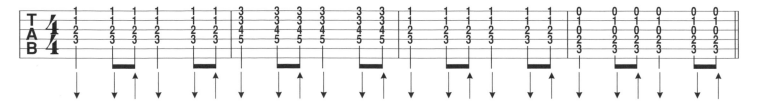

5-String Barre Chords

Bm Barre Chord

The next barre chord we'll discuss is a B minor chord based on the open-position Am chord. This chord requires a 1st-finger barre that must hold down five strings at once. Be sure to press firmly in order to securely fret each string.

To begin, arrange your 2nd, 3rd, and 4th fingers into the A minor open-position chord shape. Then, move the shape up two frets and place your 1st finger across the 2nd fret of the guitar, so that you are covering the 2nd fret from the 5th string to the 1st string:

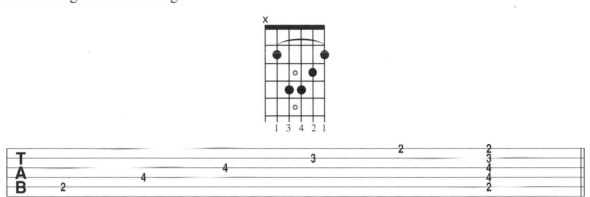

When you've become comfortable with the fingering of this chord, try switching from it to other chords you are already familiar with, such as the Bm–D progression below:

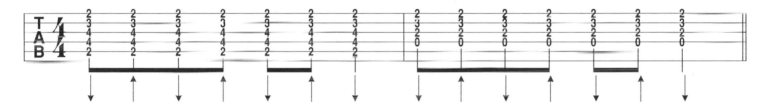

Full Barre Chords

The next barre type is called the full barre chord, which means that you bar your 1st finger across all six strings of the guitar. The full barre chord is difficult for most beginning guitarists but will become easier with practice.

G Barre Chord

Let's start with the G major full barre chord:

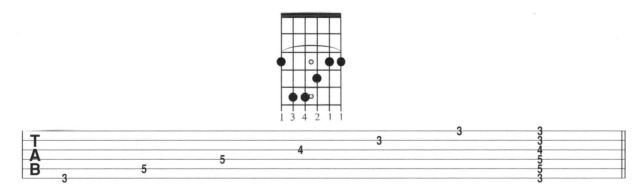

Practice the G major full barre chord using the following strumming exercise:

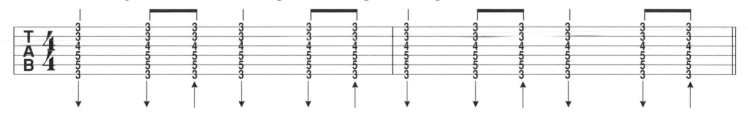

Once you're comfortable playing the full barre chord shape, try combining it with the B minor chord:

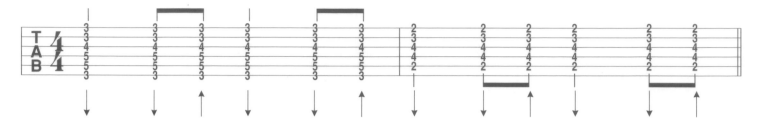

Finally, try the following chord progression, which features the G major full barre chord, the B minor barre chord, and a couple of open-position chords:

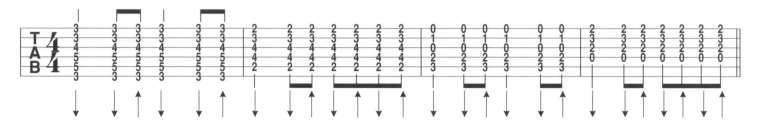

Major/Minor Barre Chord Comparisons

Let's now look at the differences between major and minor barre chords.

G/Gm Comparison

Begin by comparing the G major full barre chord that you just learned to the G minor full barre chord:

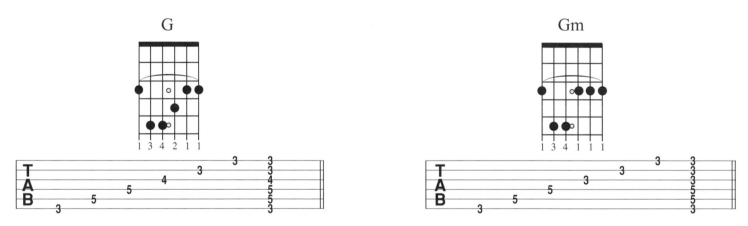

Notice that changing the G major full barre chord to the G minor full barre chord is actually simple to do; all you do is lift your 2nd finger from the 4th fret of the 4th string while keeping your 1st finger barred across the 3rd fret.

Now try this example which features the full barre chord progression from G minor to F major:

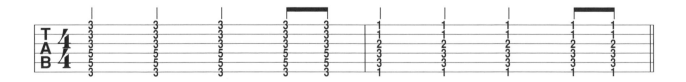

Bm/B Comparison

The next barre chord shape is based on the B minor barre chord that you already learned. The conversion from B minor to B major is similar to that of the G major/G minor, except that the B major barre chord requires that you hold down the 4th fret on the 3rd, 4th, and 5th strings:

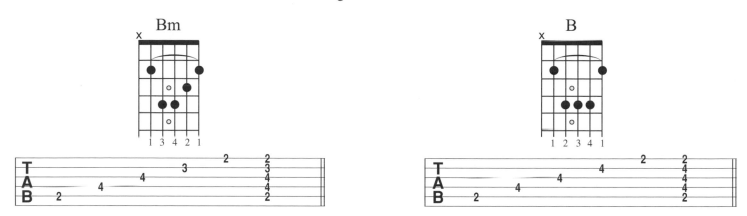

The B major barre chord can be tricky to execute cleanly at first, but with practice you can incorporate this chord for some nice-sounding progressions:

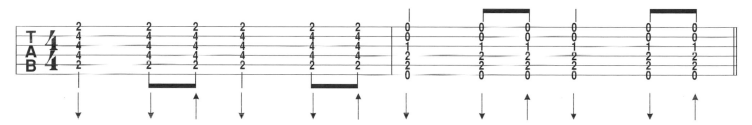

Am Open Position/Am Barre

Now let's look at using a minor barre chord shape on another area of the fretboard in order to achieve different sounds.

Let's compare an open position A minor chord to a 5th-position A minor barre chord ("5 fr." tells you the diagram starts at the 5th fret):

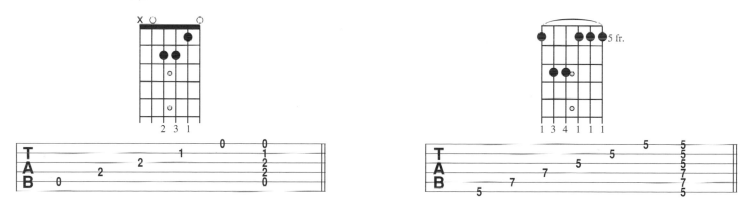

Once you're comfortable playing the A minor barre chord, play the next exercise, which combines this barre chord with the other barre chords you've learned:

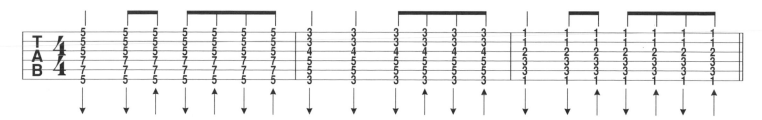

Song 11: Scarborough Fair

"Scarborough Fair" is a popular folk song that has been performed and recorded by a number of artists, most notably by 1960s American folk icons Simon and Garfunkel. The song features a combination of major and minor chords you've learned in previous chapters, as well as the use of the F major barre chord that you learned in this chapter.

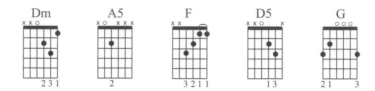

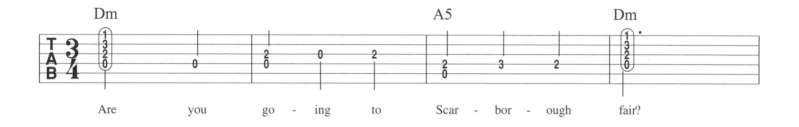

Are you go - ing to Scar - bor - ough fair?

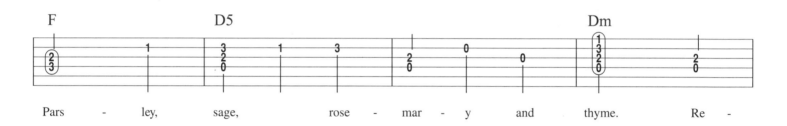

Pars - ley, sage, rose - mar - y and thyme. Re -

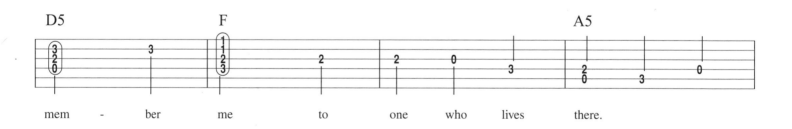

mem - ber me to one who lives there.

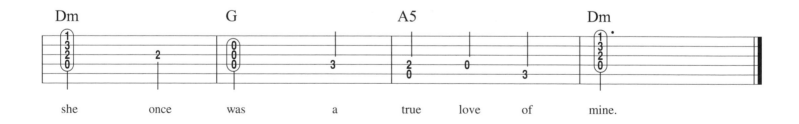

she once was a true love of mine.

Song 12: Canon in D

The following is a simplified version of Pachelbel's beloved "Canon in D," which features both the barre chords you've learned (and some new ones, for which chord diagrams have been included below), and arpeggios.

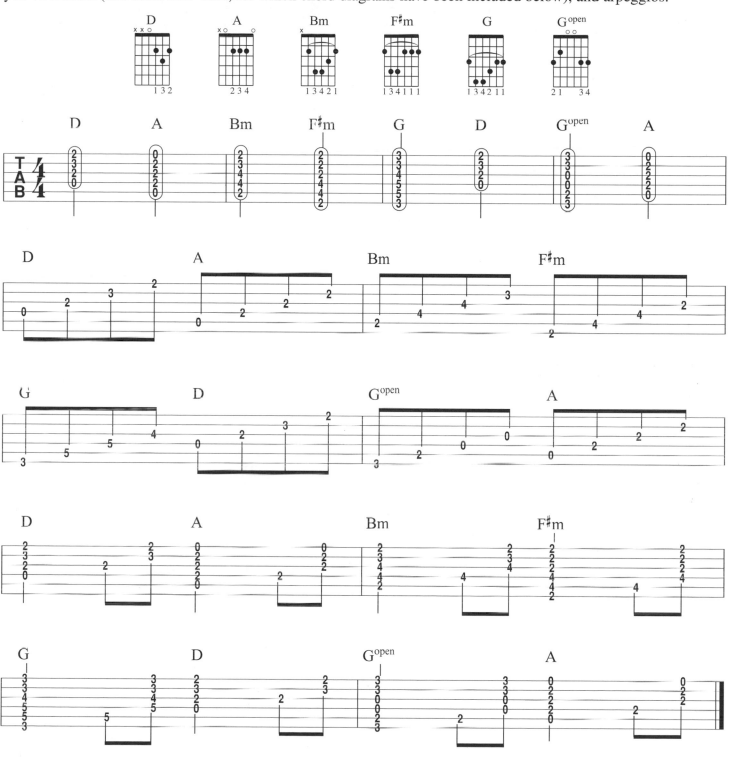

Closing Note

Now that you've made it all the way through this book, keep practicing the arpeggios, scales, and chords until playing them becomes second nature. Also take care to play according to the rhythm notation, so that you become proficient at playing in accurate time.

And a big "congratulations" to you for having taught yourself to play the guitar!

TEACH YOURSELF TO PLAY
GUITAR SONGS

Teach yourself to play your favorite songs on guitar with this multi-media learning experience! Each song in each book includes a comprehensive online video lesson with an interactive song transcription, slow-down features, looping capabilities, track choices, play-along functions, and more. The price of the books includes access to all of these online features!

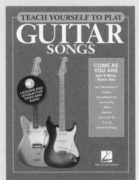

"COME AS YOU ARE" & 9 MORE ROCK HITS

Come As You Are (Nirvana) • Do I Wanna Know? (Artic Monkeys) • Heaven (Los Lonely Boys) • Here Without You (3 Doors Down) • Learn to Fly (Foo Fighters) • Plush (Stone Temple Pilots) • Santeria (Sublime) • Say It Ain't So (Weezer) • 21 Guns (Green Day) • Under the Bridge (Red Hot Chili Peppers).

Book with Online Audio & Video
00152224 .... $17.99

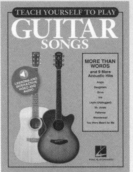

"MORE THAN WORDS" & 9 MORE ACOUSTIC HITS

Angie (The Rolling Stones) • Daughters (John Mayer) • Drive (Incubus) • Iris (Goo Goo Dolls) • Layla (Eric Clapton) • Mr. Jones (Counting Crows) • More Than Words (Extreme) • Patience (Guns N' Roses) • Wonderwall (Oasis) • You Were Meant for Me (Jewel).

Book with Online Audio & Video
00152225 .... $17.99

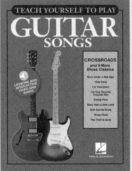

"CROSSROADS" & 9 MORE BLUES CLASSICS

Born Under a Bad Sign Albert King) • Cross Road Blues (Crossroads) (Cream) • Hide Away (Freddie King) • I'm Tore Down (Eric Clapton) • I'm Your Hoochie Coochie Man (Muddy Waters) • Killing Floor (Howlin' Wolf) • Mary Had a Little Lamb (Buddy Guy) • Still Got the Blues (Gary Moore) • Texas Flood (Stevie Ray Vaughan and Double Trouble) • The Thrill Is Gone (B.B. King).

Book with Online Audio & Video
00152183 .... $17.99

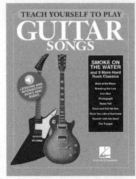

"SMOKE ON THE WATER" & 9 MORE HARD ROCK CLASSICS

Bark at the Moon (Ozzy Osbourne) • Breaking the Law (Judas Priest) • Iron Man (Black Sabbath) • Photograph (Def Leppard) • Rebel Yell (Billy Idol) • Rock and Roll All Nite (KISS) • Rock You like a Hurricane (Scorpions) • Runnin' with the Devil (Van Halen) • Smoke on the Water (Deep Purple) • The Trooper (Iron Maiden).

Book with Online Audio & Video
00152230 .... $17.99

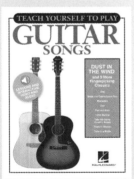

"DUST IN THE WIND" & 9 MORE FINGERPICKING CLASSICS

Anji (Simon & Garfunkel) • Babe, I'm Gonna Leave You (Led Zeppelin) • Blackbird (The Beatles) • Dee (Randy Rhoads) • Dust in the Wind (Kansas) • Fire and Rain (James Taylor) • Little Martha (The Allman Brothers Band) • Take Me Home, Country Roads (John Denver) • Tears in Heaven (Eric Clapton) • Time in a Bottle (Jim Croce).

Book with Online Audio & Video
00152184 .... $17.99

"SWEET HOME ALABAMA" & 9 MORE ROCK CLASSICS

All Right Now (Free) • The Boys Are Back in Town (Thin Lizzy) • Day Tripper (The Beatles) • Detroit Rock City (KISS) • Don't Fear the Reaper (Blue Oyster Cult) • Refugee (Tom Petty and the Heartbreakers) • Start Me Up (The Rolling Stones) • Sultans of Swing (Dire Straits) • Sweet Home Alabama (Lynyrd Skynyrd) • Walk This Way (Aerosmith).

Book with Online Audio & Video
00152181 .... $17.99